Life in an E[dwardian] Country Househo[ld]

by Mike Graham-Cameron

illustrated by Helen Herbert

Produced by Dinosaur Publications for
Cambridge University Press

Cambridge
London   New York   New Rochelle
Melbourne   Sydney

The country estate

For hundreds of years, until the First World War, country estates had been run as almost completely independent communities. At the head of each community was the person or family owning the estate. To allow the owners to live in the grand style expected of them lots of servants were needed. Indeed by about 1850, the very large estates belonging to Dukes and Earls sometimes had a small army of stewards, servants and tenants.

Each estate tried to provide its own upkeep. Nearly everything came from within its boundaries – fish and game from the rivers and fields, vegetables and herbs from the kitchen garden, milk and eggs from the home farm, fruit from the orchards. Even the timber for repairs and building was grown and felled on the estate.

This book is about an imaginary country house called Wennington Manor in the year 1900, and the family and servants who lived there.

The gamekeeper, gardener, farm manager, coachman, housekeeper, butler, cook and all the other servants helped to keep life on the estate flowing smoothly. Although they all worked for the master's family, they also had to be looked after. Every servant needed somewhere to live and clothes to wear and there were enormous amounts of food to be cooked and served. The servants worked to keep the estate in good order, and in return the master gave them a home. For many, service on an estate was their whole life.

Today, lots of estates are in the care of organisations like The National Trust or the Department of the Environment. But even privately owned houses are often open to paying visitors, which helps to provide money for the upkeep of beautiful and historic buildings.

WENNINGTON MANOR

4

Butler

Head Gardener   Lady's Maid   Cook

Nanny   Housemaid   Housemaid

Under Gardener   Stable Boy   Scullery Maid

Housekeeper

Coachman   Gamekeeper

tchen Maid   Laundry Maid   Dairymaid   Groom

Scullery Maid   Stable Boy   Footman

The housekeeper

The master of the house leaves all the domestic matters to his wife and she, in turn, gives most of the responsibility to the housekeeper.

Miss Henderson has been with the family for fifteen years and there is nothing she does not know about running the household. Sitting at her desk in the housekeeper's room, she carefully writes up the accounts. '4 sacks of flour, 2 barrels of treacle, $\frac{1}{2}$lb ginger, 3 boxes sultanas, 50 bars common soap, 1 barrel salt, 20 gallons lamp oil'. She enters the cost of each item, adds it up, closes the ledger and puts it to one side, ready to be shown to the mistress on Friday.

One of the kitchen maids knocks at the door. She has brought a list of supplies needed by cook. Miss Henderson unlocks the still-room with a key from the bunch hanging at her belt. She gives the girl some spices and coffee, and tells her to straighten her cap. Locking the door behind her, the housekeeper starts her rounds. She checks every room, including the servants' quarters, for dust and untidiness. She pauses at the linen room. Here a maid is repairing sheets with fine cotton thread, while another darns a pile of woollen socks.

Satisfied, she goes to her sitting room and rings the bell for morning coffee. After it arrives, Mr Dawson, the butler, joins her for their daily chat about the household arrangements. Between them, the housekeeper and the butler control all the other indoor servants.

The butler

In 1900 every middle class home has servants. But the number of men in service decides the importance of the household. At Wennington Manor, the head of the indoor servants is the butler, Dawson. He has many responsibilities, but most important of all he has to make sure that the guests are looked after well and that the other servants carry out their duties in the proper manner.

In the cellar of the house, Dawson lovingly surveys the racks of wine and kegs of sherry, carefully selecting bottles of claret and a fine port for tonight's dinner party. Back in the butler's pantry, he gently filters the port into a wide-bottomed decanter. He tastes the claret, pours it into crystal jugs and sets them aside to reach room temperature. He has already checked the damask tablecloths and napkins, and the maids will soon set the tables with his shining silver knives, forks, spoons and candlesticks.

Throughout the day, Dawson wears his morning suit, but at six o'clock in the evening he changes into full evening dress with tails and a black tie. Tonight he will supervise the footmen serving dinner. Standing at the side of the table, he can view the entire room by looking into the convex mirror on the opposite wall. With a discreet nod of the head, he can direct the footmen to attend to every need of the guests at the splendid meal.

The lady's maid

As the valet looks after his master's clothes, so Fraser, the lady's maid, is the personal servant of the mistress. She is an excellent needle-woman and does all the alterations and repairs to her lady's clothes. She even makes some of the gowns, and is always trimming hats with new feathers and beads. Every day she does her mistress's hair, cleverly teasing it into the latest style with curling tongs heated on a spirit lamp. Then she helps her to dress, tugging at the laces of the stays to give her lady a fashionable figure.

When her mistress is on one of her frequent visits to London or to stay with friends, Fraser packs the trunks. She is expert at folding fine cotton petticoats, underskirts, chemises, flowing nightdresses and silk stockings. She wraps velvet ball gowns in white tissue paper, selects hats and places them carefully in hatboxes, and fills the toilet case with perfumes, powders and rouge. Fraser usually travels with her mistress and has been abroad several times. She is as near to being a friend and confidante as a servant can be to her employer.

The maids

In the attics of the house sleep the maids. They have to get up at five o'clock every morning. It is usually dark outside, but before the master's family awakes, there are many jobs to be done. Yawning and stretching, they clamber out of bed and pull on their clothes.

The housemaids creep downstairs to begin their work. Some of them clean the ashes from the fireplaces of the main rooms, make the fires, light them and refill the scuttles with coal. The drawing room and the sitting rooms of the master and mistress must now be cleaned. The floors and all the massive mahogany furniture are polished with beeswax. The carpets are swept with a stiff broom, and the many ornaments are carefully dusted.

At eight o'clock the maids troop into the kitchen and collect the heavy copper cans full of hot water. They climb the back stairs from the basement and leave a can in each bedroom. They also check the pottery jug on every wash-stand to make sure it is full of clean cold water. Later they empty the slops, clean the wash bowls and struggle downstairs with the heavy buckets of dirty water.

At eight-thirty, breakfast is brought into the dining room. The maids are busy carrying the warmed dishes of porridge, kidneys, bacon, kedgeree, eggs, kippers and tomatoes to the sideboard. They put steaming pots of delicious-smelling coffee and silver racks of toast on the table. The family assembles, and with lowered eyes, they and the servants stand in silence while the master says morning prayers, before the family begin their meal.

For much of the day, the maids are busy. There are beds to be made, staircases and hallways to be swept, dusted and polished, tables to be laid and cleared and meals to be served. There are breaks for breakfast, lunch and tea, but by ten o'clock at night Jessie, the house-maid, is thankful to change into her long nightgown and to slide exhausted between the sheets before blowing out the candle.

Nanny

Over the years Nanny has comforted, scolded and generally looked after eighteen children in two generations of the master's family. Every day she supervises their routine, looking after them for the mistress until the boys are old enough to go to boarding school and the girls to be educated by their governess.

Master William and Miss Alice, out on their daily walk, run ahead as Nanny pushes Anna, the baby, in her big black pram along the gravelled path. They rush indoors and up the stairs to the nursery where tea is ready, but they must wait for Nanny before they can begin. Nanny eats many of her meals with the children, making sure that they don't gobble or talk with their mouths full. She is very strict about table manners.

When the nursery maid has cleared the table and is getting the bath ready, the children clamber onto Nanny's cosy lap. She reads them a story, showing them the pictures as she turns over each page.

Master William squeals as Nanny washes behind his ears with a rough flannel. She finishes bathing him and rubs him dry with a huge white towel which has been warmed in front of the fire. Baby Anna whimpers in her cradle. Nanny gently rocks it, singing nursery rhymes to soothe her back to sleep.

At last, the young children say their prayers and are tucked up in bed. The mistress comes in to kiss them goodnight, and to talk for a while about the children's day.

Cook

In the huge kitchen there is a bustle of activity. Copper pans bubble on the hobs of the black iron stove. Steam rises to the high ceiling where herbs, legs of ham and sides of bacon hang. In the centre of the room are two large scrubbed tables. Mrs Woodruff, the cook, plump and perspiring, is rolling out pastry with expert hands and shouting instructions to the two kitchen maids. One is slicing a heap of carrots and swedes. The other is surrounded by flying feathers as she quickly plucks half a dozen partridges.

In the scullery, leading off the kitchen, Ethel, the new scullery maid, pauses in scrubbing the grease from a huge baking tin to wipe her nose on the back of her hand.

Ever since Cook came down to the kitchen after discussing the day's menu with the mistress, they have been preparing for this evening's dinner party. Puddings have already been baked and decorated, cold meats garnished, fish gutted and sauces mixed.

Cook opens one of the oven doors, checks the roasting crown of lamb and quickly slides in the tray of flan cases. Calling over her shoulder, she tells one of the maids to stoke up the range. The housekeeper comes down to make sure that everything is going to be ready on time. She has a few words with Mrs Woodruff and admires the puddings laid out in the cold room. Well-paid and over-worked, Mrs Woodruff is one of the most important people in the household. In her vast white apron, she rules supreme in the kitchen. No-one dares to annoy her, not even the housekeeper.

The laundry maids

Ellen, the head laundry maid, lifts the lid of the huge copper, and furiously stabs at the boiling mass of sheets and pillowcases with a long wooden paddle. Mountains of dirty washing are piled into wicker baskets on the floor – shirts, petticoats, vests, drawers, nightshirts, socks, table linen, caps, cuffs, collars, dresses and pinafores.

Next, using the big mangle, she squeezes the water out of some freshly washed towels, before pegging them up on the line in the yard. She is in a hurry. It is a fine windy day and she hopes to get all the washing dry before sundown.

At the far end of the laundry, flat-irons are heating up on the range ready for young Liza to do the pressing. Each iron is numbered with its weight in pounds and is used in turn until it cools down. The frills and flounces on ladies' petticoats and maids' caps must be starched and crimped using special fluting irons like tiny mangles with cogs instead of rollers.

Every day, except Sunday, is washing day at Wennington Manor, and at spring cleaning time, all the blankets and curtains must be washed too.

The dairy maid

Across the yard in the dairy, Kate rubs her hands together to try and warm them. The dairy is always cold, because otherwise the milk would not keep fresh, and Kate wishes she could stop shivering. She has been up since five o'clock to scrub the stone-flagged floor and utensils. They must be spotlessly clean before the milk arrives from the home farm.

At 6 o'clock the farm cart clatters into the yard and Jim carries the heavy milk churns into the dairy. He plonks them on the floor and drives off, whistling. Kate pours the milk into shallow separating dishes which she puts aside till next day. Meanwhile she carefully skims pints of cream from the top of milk that has been standing since yesterday. She pours it into the butter churn. She grasps the handle and begins to turn it. Round and round and round she churns, until her arms ache and still the cream has not thickened into butter.

She sighs and sits down for a few moments. The kitchen maid comes into the dairy and collects a pitcher of milk for the cook. Slowly Kate turns the handle of the butter churn again, and before long she can feel that the thick yellow butter is beginning to form. She scoops it out onto a marble slab, and using two wooden butter pats, expertly shapes it into neat oblongs. Several of these she cuts into small pieces and, deftly using the two butter pats, rolls them into neat butter balls the size of marbles. These will be used at the dinner table.

The coachman

Joshua, the coachman, rolls down his sleeves, pulls on his best boots, struggles into his green uniform and adjusts his top hat with its smart cockade. Taking his whip from its stand he strides into the yard to inspect the elegant coach. The four magnificent draw horses, sleekly groomed with their brasses shining, are already harnessed to the carriage.

The master and his family are invited for luncheon at the Castle, and Joshua is driving them there in a few minutes. All morning the grooms have been combing and brushing the horses' glossy coats and the stable boys have been polishing the harness. The horses were fed on horse beans this morning so they are "full of beans", impatiently stamping on the cobbles with their iron-shod hooves, tossing their heads and snorting.

Joshua mounts the box and drives the coach round to the front of the house where the two footmen help the master and his family into the comfortable leather seats. They close the doors and climb up onto the back. The coachman cracks his whip and the horses strain forwards. The heavy coach begins to move, slowly gathering speed until it is swaying down the driveway at a fine pace.

The gardeners

In a corner of the large, walled kitchen garden, Melrose, the head gardener, finishes instructing one of the under-gardeners how to plant out the boxes of lettuce seedlings. As he turns away and walks towards the strawberry beds, he checks that the herb garden has been properly weeded. He plucks a sprig of rosemary and rubs it between his fingers, smelling the sweet scent with satisfaction.

On the terrace of the house, another gardener is shovelling leaf mould and horse manure into great ornamental stone urns. When planted with geraniums, they will make bright splashes of colour – pink and red – all summer long.

Having arranged the work of the under-gardeners, Melrose goes into the conservatory to tend the collection of exotic tropical plants. Palms, ferns, bamboo trees and waxen orchids flourish luxuriantly in the humid glass and cast-iron building.

Many of the vegetables and most of the fruit for the house come from Wennington's own gardens. Loganberries, asparagus, artichokes, peaches, apples, pears, carrots, turnips, peas, beans, pumpkins and plenty more, grow under the skilful care of Melrose and his assistants. He is responsible for all the cultivated grounds, except for the farm. Melrose is rightly proud of the gardens at Wennington Manor, which are the envy of the neighbouring estates.

The gamekeeper

Dickson, the head gamekeeper, strolls into the kitchen and dumps three brace of pheasant on the chopping block. Cook bustles over and inspects them approvingly. While she gives him a warming cup of beef tea, he sits in a chair by the range and tells her what meat and fish she can soon expect from the estate lands. The master has asked him to organise another shoot for the coming week and six 'Guns', nobility and gentry, are expected.

The kitchen relies on Dickson to provide a lot of the fish and meat for the household, and with the help of two assistant keepers, he looks after the game on the whole estate. Trout and salmon, pheasant, partridges, grouse, pigeons, hares and rabbits are all part of his responsibility, as well as the small herd of deer which provides venison for special occasions.

Just lately, Dickson has been worried about the number of pheasants which have been taken by poachers, and as he strides across towards the spinney, he hears the report of a shotgun. No-one from the estate is out shooting this evening. It must be poachers!

He runs towards the trees, stops for a moment to load two cartridges into his gun and dashes forward again shouting, "Come out, you varmints. I know you're in there!" With a crashing of the undergrowth and a flurry of frightened game birds, two figures dash from cover and sprint away into the gloom. Dickson stands, and carefully aiming low, fires both barrels, peppering their backsides with shot. They are scarcely hurt and carry on running. But Dickson knows they are shaken enough to keep away for a month or two.

The farm hands

Haymaking is always a busy time at Wennington home farm. Duncan Brown and his ten farm workers rise at daybreak and with hired villagers helping, they scythe down the tall grass. Using long pitchforks, they turn it over to dry in the sun.

Some days later, when it is quite dry, they load it onto the big wooden haywain ready to be carted away and made into hay stacks. It is hot and dusty work and when Mrs Brown brings a huge hamper of cheese and fresh-baked bread together with stone jars of home made ale and cider, everyone is glad to sit on the ground to eat dinner and have a rest.

Duncan is anxious to get the hay stacked before it rains. The home farm cattle will feed on it throughout the winter. More than half the milk produced by the dairy herd is sold to the villagers, the rest goes to Wennington Manor. Apart from dairy cattle, Wennington has sheep and a beef herd. These provide meat for the house as well as being sold to butchers in the nearby market town. Wool from the sheep is sent away to be spun and woven into cloth. The income produced by the farm is very important to the Master, because it helps him to buy goods which cannot be provided from within the estate.

There is always work to be done on the farm, but the most important time is the harvest at the end of the summer. Duncan has a hundred and forty acres of grain crops, and this year for the first time, he will use a mechanical threshing machine driven by the new steam traction engine.

Entertainments

Life 'below stairs' was often very tiring but there was fun too. One of the happiest times was Christmas when presents were given by the master's family to their servants. Usually the girls received cloth to make into dresses and the men were given money. The celebrations reached a peak with the Servants' Ball. The master would start the dancing with the housekeeper, and then everyone would join in to the music from the piano and perhaps a violin and concertina. All the maids would be prettily dressed, while the menservants, with their hair well-brushed, would be wearing their best suits. A long table, groaning with Christmas fare and gallons of beer and ale, would be surrounded by laughing, merry-making people.

Many servants spent all their lives with one family, like the boy who started work at the age of 8, scaring birds from the crops on the estate farm, and died an old man have reached the important position of head groom.

Few working people in 1900 had an easy life, but compared to those who toiled in the thousands of huge factories in industrial towns, the life of a man or girl "in service" was quite good, and in some cases, very happy.

There are many good examples of the work-places of servants, all preserved for visitors to see. Some of the most interesting are listed below:

Charlecote Park, Wellesbourne, Warwickshire
Brewery, coaches, kitchen.

Erdigg House, Wrexham, North Wales
Joinery workshop, servants' hall, portraits of servants.

Cotehele, Calstock, Nr Tavistock, Cornwall
Dovecote, watermill, audio-visual slides on how the estates worked.

Llanhydrock, Bodmin, Cornwall
Dairy, Kitchen, bakery.

Hardwick Hall, Nr Mansfield, Derbyshire
Kitchen, herb garden.

Blickling Hall, Blickling, Norwich

Felbrigg Hall, Felbrigg, Cromer, Norfolk
Kitchen.